Leaders of Religion
MUHAMMAD

Dilwyn Hunt M.A.

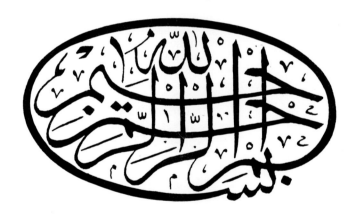

OLIVER & BOYD

Acknowledgements

The author and publishers wish to thank Amena Pictures Ltd for permission to reproduce the photograph on the inside back cover.

Illustrated by Joanna Troughton

Oliver & Boyd
Longman House
Burnt Mill
Harlow
Essex CM20 2JE

An Imprint of Longman Group UK Ltd

ISBN 0 05 003913 X

First Published 1985
Eighth impression 1993

Typeset in Linotron 202 Palatino and Helvetica
Produced by Longman Singapore Publishers Pte Ltd
Printed in Singapore

The publisher's policy is to use paper manufactured
from sustainable forests.

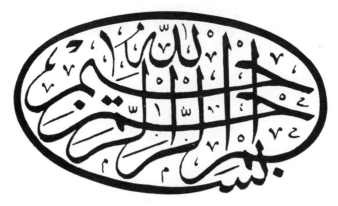

This piece of decorative script is called the
Bismillah. It means 'In the name of God'.

CONTENTS

		page
	Introduction	4
1	The Days of Ignorance	6
2	The Night of Power	10
3	The Prophet Speaks	16
4	The Desperate Years	22
5	The City of the Prophet	27
6	Victory at Badr	30
7	The Years of Growth	35
8	Triumph at Last	40
9	'Most Noble of all Creation'	47

INTRODUCTION

In a number of world religions certain people are regarded as the great leaders or teachers of that religion. Some of these people are called Founders because it was largely through their efforts that a new religion began. Jesus of Nazareth for example, is often called the Founder of Christianity. Gautama, the Buddha, was the Founder of Buddhism. In Judaism, although there are many great leaders including Abraham, Jacob and Joseph, for most Jewish people the greatest of them all is Moses.

In the religion of Islam no one is given the title Founder. Some people have mistakenly called Muhammad the 'Founder of Islam' but to the millions of people who follow the faith, Islam began with God (Allah). God first revealed Islam to Adam and later the faith was revealed to many other Messengers or Prophets of God. The last and greatest of these Prophets is Muhammad. It is with Muhammad that the faith was completed. Followers of Islam (they are called Muslims) believe that Muhammad is the 'Seal of the Prophets'.

This book looks at the story of this great man, Muhammad.

SOME PROPHETS OF ISLAM

ADAM (Adam)
IDRIS (Enoch)
NUH (Noah)
HUD
SALIH
IBRAHIM (Abraham)
ISMAIL (Ishmael)
ISHAQ (Isaac)
LUT (Lot)
YAQUB (Jacob)
YUSUF (Joseph)
SHUAYB
AYYUB (Job)
MUSA (Moses)
HARUN (Aaron)
DHUL-KIFL (Ezekiel)
DAWUD (David)
SULAYMAN (Solomon)
ILAS (Elias)
AL-YASA (Elisha)
YUNUS (Jonah)
ZAKARIYYA (Zechariah)
YAHYA (John)
ISA (Jesus)
MUHAMMAD

4

Muslims do not believe Muhammad or his closest friends should be drawn or represented in any way. For this reason, in this book you will find Muhammad does not appear in any of the plays, nor are any pictures drawn of him.

All the newspaper articles and radio programmes in this book are of course imaginary and even the plays should not be thought to be attempts to reconstruct past events exactly. Their purpose is to introduce readers in a lively and appealing way to one of the world's great religions, Islam, and the life of the Prophet Muhammad, a man revered by millions.

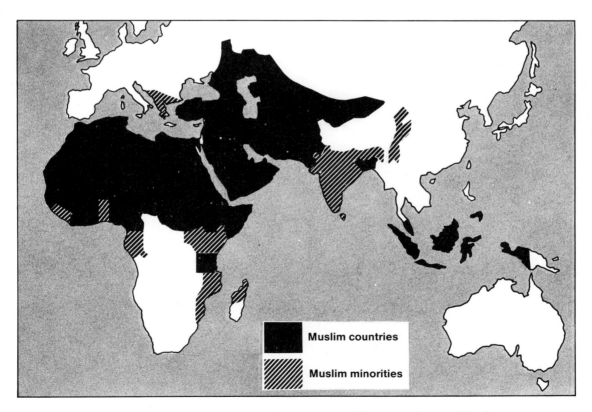

Map showing the countries where most of the people are Muslims. It also shows the countries where there are large numbers of Muslims, although they are still a minority of the population.

UNIT 1

The Days of Ignorance

Muhammad was born about 571 CE, in the country of Arabia, in the city of Mecca (Makkah). In those days, most Arabs worshipped many gods. They made idols or statues of their gods and housed them in shrines of which the most important was in Mecca itself. This shrine was a large, cube-shaped building called the Ka'ba (Ka'bah). Inside and on top of this shrine were kept over three hundred and sixty idols. Great fairs were held at Mecca and people would come from all over the country to worship at the Ka'ba.

'And their worship at the holy House
is naught but whistling and hand-clapping...'
(The Qur'an, Surah 8, verse 35.)

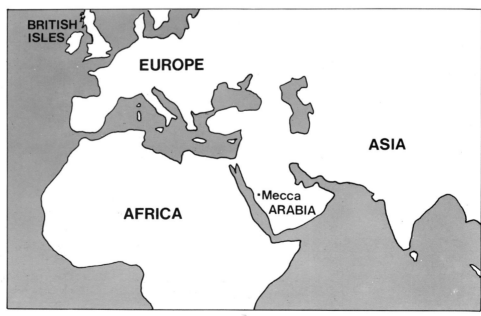

Map showing the location of Mecca, where Muhammad was born.

Mecca was not only famous as a religious centre but also as the business centre of Arabia. In the city lived many wealthy merchants who organised the buying and selling of goods. These people were clever but sadly they seemed to have very little care for anyone apart from themselves. In Arabia at that time there were many desperately poor people but the rich merchants of Mecca did nothing to help them. They showed no generosity towards others but only used their wealth to make more money for themselves. Often arrogant and self-centred, living lives of luxury, they didn't even take their gods very seriously. Power and wealth were their idols.

Before Muhammad began preaching, most of the people of Arabia lived in ignorance of the belief in one God. For this reason, Muslims call this age 'the Days of Ignorance'. Although most Arabs worshipped many gods, there were some who worshipped one God. For example, various Christian communities were scattered around Arabia and also some tribes believed in the religion of Judaism. In the sacred book of Islam, the Qur'an, there are also frequently mentioned people who are called the 'Hanif' or 'the searchers for the truth'. The Hanif believed in neither Christianity nor Judaism but are described as followers of the true religion, the pure worship of God.

'Nay, but ye (for your part) honour not the orphan. And urge not on the feeding of the poor. And ye devour heritages with devouring greed. And love wealth with abounding love.'
(The Qur'an, Surah 89, verses 17–20.)

What have you remembered?

1. Muslims believe that the last and greatest messenger of God is:

   | Jesus | Moses | Muhammad | Abraham |

2. Muhammad was born in the country of:

   | Persia | Egypt | India | Arabia |

3. Muhammad was born in the city of:

   | Mecca | Medina | Bethlehem | Jerusalem |

4. Before Muhammad preached about God, in the Ka'ba shrine there was kept:

   | nothing | a tomb | one idol | over 360 idols |

5. Before Muhammad preached about God, most people in Arabia worshipped:

   | one God | many gods | Christ | Hanif |

Complete the sentences. Match the phrases in the left-hand column with the words from the right.

6.	The rich merchants of Mecca showed little	Hanif
7.	Statues of gods are called	luxury
8.	In ancient Arabia there were many people who were desperately	generosity
9.	In ancient Arabia a person who worshipped one God, a searcher for truth, was called a	idols
10.	The rich merchants of Mecca lived lives of	poor

8

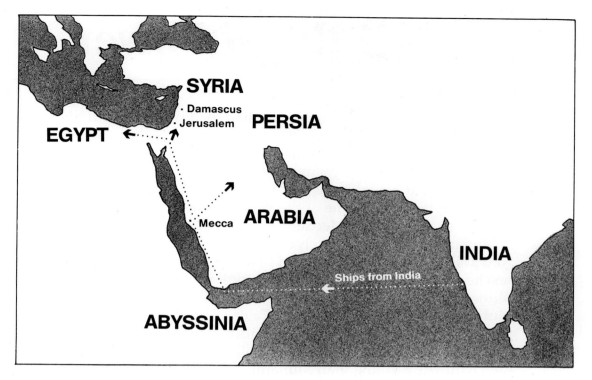

Map showing the main trade routes through Arabia at the time of Muhammad.

What do you know?

11. Whom do Muslims call the 'Seal of the Prophets'?
12. Why were the pilgrimages to the Ka'ba and the great fairs so important for the business life of Mecca? (The map will help you here.)

What do you think?

13. Some people have said that the merchants of Mecca are like many people today. Do you think this is true? If so, in what way do you think there are similarities?
14. Muslims refer to life in Arabia before Muhammad as 'the Days of Ignorance'. Ignorance of what, do you think?

The Night of Power

Muhammad's father died before Muhammad was born and his mother died when he was six years old. Left an orphan, he was brought up first by his grandfather and then later by his uncle, Abu Talib. Abu Talib, like so many other people in Mecca at that time, was a merchant but his business was very small. He was a well respected citizen but he was not one of the very rich merchants who had become so powerful in Mecca.

Muhammad was only twelve, we are told, when he was taken by Abu Talib on a business trip. On that trip when the camel caravan reached Busra in Syria, a Christian monk named Bahira saw Muhammad and questioned him. When he had finished questioning Muhammad, Bahira went to Abu Talib. 'Guard him carefully,' Bahira warned, 'a great future lies before this nephew of yours.'

When he was older, Muhammad, like his uncle, became a merchant. As a young man Muhammad gained a reputation for reliability and honesty and was nicknamed, 'al-Amin' which means 'the trustworthy one.'

At about the age of twenty-five, a widow called Khadija put Muhammad in charge of some of her business deals. He carried out the work so well that he won the admiration and later the affection of Khadija and so they married. From the time of his marriage until he started preaching, Muhammad lived in Mecca and although the business did well, they were never very rich.

During this time Muhammad slowly began to change. Like the Christians and the Jews, he came to feel that the idol-worship of his fellow Arabs was wrong and he began to think more and more about belief in one God. Also, the poverty of many Arabs and the wastefulness of many of the rich merchants made Muhammad increasingly unhappy. He liked to retreat to the mountains outside Mecca to think deeply and to try to find the answers to the questions which were troubling his mind. His retreats into the mountains grew longer, sometimes lasting several days. During one of these retreats something extraordinary took place.

'Say (O Muhammad): . . . And the Qur'an hath been inspired in me, that I may warn therewith you and whomsoever it may reach . . .'

(The Qur'an Surah 6, verse 19.)

10

It happened when Muhammad was aged about forty, in the year 610 CE. He was in a cave on Mount Hira, just outside Mecca. It was dark and he had already been on the mountain for several days. Suddenly something appeared to him. Muhammad's heart raced with fear...there in front of him stood the angel Gabriel. Words appeared and Muhammad was commanded to read.

> **'Read! In the name of your Lord**
> **Who created man from a clot of blood**
> **Read! And your Lord is the Most Gracious One**
> **Who taught by the pen**
> **Who taught mankind what he did not know.'**
> (The Qur'an, Surah 96, verses 1–5.)

Muslims believe that Muhammad could not read. Nevertheless, these words became as though written on Muhammad's heart. They are the first verses revealed to Muhammad from God. Over the next twenty-three years of his life, Muhammad received many more revelations like this. The revelations were written down as they were sent, and formed the sacred book of Islam, the Qur'an. Every year Muslims remember when this first revelation came. They call it 'the Night of Power'.

> **'Lo! We revealed it on the Night of Power.**
> **And what will make you know what the Night of Power is?**
> **The Night of Power is better than a thousand months**
> **In it the angels and the Spirit [Gabriel] descend by permission of their Lord with every Command.**
> **Peace it is until the rising of the Dawn.'**
> (The Qur'an, Surah 97, verses 1–5.)

Abu Talib's Decision

Cast: Abu Talib   Muhammad's eldest uncle and leader of his family
Abu Lahab   Muhammad's uncle and bitter opponent
Hamza   Muhammad's uncle. He is quite sympathetic towards Islam.
'Abbas   Muhammad's uncle and a very wealthy merchant

Scene: Mecca, about 610 CE. Muhammad has just started to preach and so the head of Muhammad's family, Abu Talib, calls a meeting of the family's elders to make a difficult decision.

ABU TALIB: Ah...there you are Hamza. We've been waiting for you. Sit down. Well, apart from Hamza, we have all listened to Muhammad and I for one would say that I have never heard anyone so certain of themselves or speaking so beautifully. Hamza, you have really missed something extraordinary.

ABU LAHAB: Yes, yes, Abu Talib...enough of that. Why are we here?

'ABBAS: Why? Well...I would have thought that was obvious. As leaders of the family we have to decide whether Muhammad is to have the protection of his family.

ABU TALIB: That's right 'Abbas, but I'm head of the family and I will have to decide. I've called you all here so that I can hear what you've all got to say.

HAMZA: What's all this about? Why should Muhammad lose his family's protection?

ABU LAHAB: If you had been here on time, Hamza, you would know what your stupid nephew has been up to.

ABU TALIB: Hamza, you know that Muhammad for some time has been going up into the mountains...

ABU LAHAB: Crazy!

HAMZA: He's not crazy. Our own father, every year, did the same thing.

ABU LAHAB: Muhammad is different. He says that on the mountains God speaks to him.

'ABBAS: He says all our gods are nothing, bits of wood and stone. They're not real according to him.

HAMZA: So what? There are others in this city who don't believe in the gods. Do *you* really believe in those gods, 'Abbas? You think more about making money than you do about the gods.

ABU LAHAB: That's not the point. 'Abbas keeps his views to himself, Muhammad doesn't. He's been going around the city preaching. He wants to change people.

ABU TALIB: He says this God puts words into his mind and has commanded him to teach those words. He thinks he's a messenger of God, a prophet.

HAMZA: Muhammad wouldn't lie.

ABU LAHAB: You can't believe what he says.

HAMZA: I didn't say that. I said, Muhammad wouldn't lie. I've never known a man to be so honest.

ABU LAHAB: Then he's crazy. Are we going to carry on protecting someone who is mad?

HAMZA: Who's crazy in this world, Abu Lahab? You, with your jewels and your smart friends, or Muhammad because he's honest and doesn't care about having a big house or expensive clothes?

ABU TALIB: Hamza's right. I know Muhammad better than any of you. I brought him up from when he was just a small boy. He wouldn't lie. You heard him yourself. . .he believes what he says is true. Muhammad will keep the protection of his family.

ABU LAHAB: Well, I'll not help him. My own son is married to Muhammad's daughter. If he carries on like this I will make sure they are divorced.

HAMZA: You wouldn't dare turn your back on your own flesh and blood.

ABU LAHAB: Just watch me! Every merchant in the city will rise up against Muhammad. Wealth, business and the gods run Mecca, not a messenger from God.

ABU TALIB: What about you 'Abbas? You've been very quiet.

ABBAS: Muhammad is family...we must protect him, but Abu Lahab is right. The chief citizens of Mecca will not like what Muhammad is saying.

HAMZA: We will deal with that problem — if it arises.

ABU LAHAB: When it arises.

ABU TALIB: That's settled then. Muhammad will continue to have the protection of the family. If any man hurts him he will be revenged.

ABBAS: Let's hope it doesn't come to that.

ABU LAHAB: Crazy — you're all crazy!

What have you remembered?

Complete the sentences in the left-hand column with the words from the right.

1.	By the age of six Muhammad was an	Power
2.	As a young man Muhammad was nicknamed the	Khadija
3.	In his first revelation Muhammad believed he saw the angel	read
4.	People who believe in Islam are called	orphan
5.	Muhammad's first wife was named	uncle
6.	To think and be alone Muhammad would spend time outside Mecca in the	trustworthy one
7.	The sacred book of Islam is the	Gabriel
8.	The first revelation Muhammad had took place on the Night of	Muslims
9.	After his grandfather died Muhammad was brought up by his	Qur'an
10.	At his first revelation words appeared in front of Muhammad and he was commanded to	mountains

What do you know?

11. About how old was Muhammad when he had his first revelation of the Qur'an?
12. Was Muhammad born before or after Jesus of Nazareth?
13. Roughly how many years separate the two men?
14. Life in Mecca was making Muhammad increasingly unhappy. Why?
15. Like the Christians and the Jews, what did Muhammad come to believe in?
16. To stop Muhammad preaching what did Muhammad's uncle, Abu Lahab, threaten to do?
17. What did the leader of Muhammad's family, Abu Talib, decide to do which was of great help to Muhammad?
18. The response of each of his four uncles to Muhammad's belief that God had spoken to him was slightly different. Describe the reaction of two of his uncles and try to explain the reasons why they thought as they did.
19. Every year Muslims remember 'the Night of Power'. Try to find out how they remember this special occasion.

What do you think?

20. Muslims believe the revelation of the Qur'an was a miracle. Why do you think they believe this?
21. Do you think the description of Muhammad's first revelation is similar to any event in life of any other great leader of religion? If so, describe this event and say how you think the two are similar.

The Prophet Speaks

Under the protection of his family Muhammad preached in Mecca and slowly Islam began to grow. Many people found that what Muhammad had to say meant a great deal to them. Some felt ashamed, some felt guilty and some felt angry.

Muhammad claimed there was only one God and that there were obvious signs of God everywhere — in the beauty of nature, in life-giving water, in the growth of crops and in the miracle of birth. Muhammad said he had been called to remind people of God and to serve as God's messenger. All the other gods worshipped at the Ka'ba and at other shrines were false and should be destroyed.

'All that is in the heavens and all that is in the earth glorifieth Allah . . .'
(The Qur'an, Surah 64, verse 1.)

Probably few Arabs at that time believed in a life after death. But Muhammad told them to think seriously about death and what they were doing with their lives. He said that there was more to life than comfort, luxury or money-making. There were people who should be helped, like orphans, widows, the sick, the diseased and the hungry. Muhammad warned that God would judge every person's life and that there was a reward for those who lived their lives properly. He also warned that for those who had not given a thought for God or for others but who had pleased only themselves, there would be no reward. There would be only a punishment.

Many of the things Muhammad said seemed totally new to the Arabs. He said that wars and feuds should stop and quarrels should be settled through laws. Those who became Muslims, he said, were equal to one another because God judged everyone in the same way, whatever their colour, tribe or nation.

None of these ideas pleased the rich merchants of Mecca. If people stopped believing in the idols, as Muhammad told them, then they would not worship at the Ka'ba. This meant that fewer goods would be sold at the great fairs. The merchants also believed that Muhammad's claim to be God's messenger meant that Muhammad, and not themselves, should be the ruler of Mecca.

At first the merchants didn't take Muhammad very seriously but as more people became Muslims they decided they had better stop him. They called him a liar. They insulted him and laughed at him in the streets. They even went to Muhammad's uncle, Abu Talib, and told him that he must stop Muhammad. However, Abu Talib bravely stuck to his decision to stand by his nephew.

'And when they see thee (O Muhammad) they treat thee only as a jest (saying): Is this he whom Allah sendeth as a messenger?'
(The Qur'an Surah 25, verse 41.)

17

Hamza becomes a Muslim

Cast: Hamza: One of Muhammad's uncles
        Abu Jahl: A rich merchant and a bitter enemy of Muhammad
        Abu Sufyan: A rich merchant and one of the chief citizens of Mecca
        Hind: The wife of Abu Sufyan

Scene: About 612 CE. Abu Jahl, a rich merchant, has insulted Muhammad. Hamza, Muhammad's uncle, in a furious temper decides to avenge his nephew. He finds Abu Jahl with his friends beside the Ka'ba.

ABU JAHL: Well, Hamza...what are you looking so angry about? Don't tell me your nephew has told you off about your wine drinking? Ha ha!..., (*Everyone except Hamza laughs.*)

HAMZA: You have insulted Muhammad.

ABU JAHL: Me, Hamza? No...we might have had a little disagreement...

HAMZA: It was no little disagreement, Abu Jahl. You called an honest man a liar, you...

ABU JAHL: Muhammad is a liar. He is a menace to this city. He would ruin our business and...aaahh! (*Hamza hits Abu Jahl.*)

HAMZA: Don't ever insult him, Abu Jahl, for I swear if you do you will answer to me. (*Members of Abu Jahl's tribe move forward to strike Hamza.*)

HAMZA: Come on then...if you dare! Hit me!

ABU JAHL: Leave him alone...he's right, I did insult Muhammad.

HAMZA: Muhammad's religion is my religion. Do you hear that? I am with Muhammad...what he says, I say, and if you fight against him then you will fight against me. (*Hamza angrily walks off.*)

ABU SUFYAN: That's done it, Hamza is now a Muslim.

HIND: He is a dangerous man...one of the bravest warriors in Mecca.

ABU JAHL: We must do something about these Muslims. We're too soft with them. They insult our gods and Muhammad mocks our way of life. He says give to the poor, feed the hungry, free our slaves. Does Muhammad think we're made of money? He says we will live again after we die...what nonsense!

HIND: Shut up Abu Jahl! We all know Muhammad is a nuisance but we must think of a sensible way of dealing with him.

ABU JAHL: A nuisance! Is that all you've got to say? Muhammad has divided our families, father against son, brother against sister. Hind, your own brother is one of them. Your family should have had Hudayfah beaten.

ABU SUFYAN: Please...how can we fight Muhammad when we fight amongst ourselves? We should easily be able to put Muhammad down. If we refuse to trade with him, how long do you think he can go on for? He has already lost what little money he had. He will have to give in.

19

HIND:	We could ruin his friend Abu Bakr. He has already lost half his fortune buying slaves and giving them their freedom.
ABU JAHL:	Too soft! You're all too soft! The main pilgrimage will be in two months. If Muhammad is still preaching that the gods of the Ka'ba are false, who knows how many pilgrims he will convince and so how many customers we will lose? We must ruin Muhammad's name so that no one will believe him.
ABU SUFYAN:	That's not a bad idea. We could say that he was possessed by a demon or that he was sick in the head.
ABU JAHL:	We must do more than that. We must torture Muhammad's followers and make them give up this nonsense.
HIND:	Muhammad and some of his followers are protected by their family but there are Muslims who have no protection.
ABU JAHL:	You mean slaves and those with no tribe...yes, we could torture them.
ABU SUFYAN:	We could talk to them.
ABU JAHL:	Bah! Talk, talk! Where does it get you? We should torture them.

What have you remembered?

True or False Which box has the true answer in it?

1. Muhammad said that there was | one God | many gods |

2. Muhammad said there was | life after death | no life after death |

3. Muhammad said he was | God's son | God's messenger |

4. Muhammad told the people to | worship the gods of the Ka'ba | destroy the idols kept in the Ka'ba |

5. Muhammad said everyone should | spend money only on themselves | help the sick |

6. Muhammad said that God would judge everyone's life and He would

reward some and punish others	return everyone to life again on earth

7. The merchants of Mecca said that everything Muhammad taught

he made up himself	came from God

8. When they heard Muhammad preaching, the Meccan merchants would

listen to him very seriously	laugh at him and insult him

9. The Meccan merchants called Muhammad

a liar	the Prophet of God

10. Muhammad's uncle Hamza

became a Muslim	bitterly opposed Islam all his life

What do you know?

11. The Meccan merchants believed that Muhammad's preaching could ruin their lives. Why did they think this?
12. Apart from laughing at him and insulting him, why were the merchants of Mecca not prepared to attack or torture Muhammad himself?
13. In the play, 'Hamza becomes a Muslim' we are told that one of Muhammad's closest friends, Abu Bakr, had 'already lost half his fortune'. Why had Abu Bakr lost so much money?

What do you think?

14. Before Muhammad, there were many feuds in Arabia. What are feuds and why do you think they can sometimes lead to the death of many people?
15. Muslims believe that there are obvious signs in nature that prove that God is real. What sort of things are there in nature, do you think, that make people believe in God?
16. Do you think nature in any way proves God is real? If so try and explain why.

The Desperate Years

As Islam grew, the chief citizens of Mecca decided to take stronger action. Some Muslims were locked up, others were not given food or water and a few were beaten. A black slave called Bilal, for example, was cruelly tortured by his owner. Umayya, his owner, had Bilal taken into the burning desert and ordered a huge rock to be placed on his chest. But Bilal would not give in. Abu Bakr, Muhammad's close friend, was so impressed by Bilal's courage that he bought the slave and gave him his freedom. Not everyone was so lucky. A Muslim women called Sumaiyya was tortured to death, but even as she died she refused to give up her faith.

'Our Lord! Make us not a prey for those who disbelieve, and forgive us, our Lord!'
(The Qur'an, Surah 40, verse 5.)

Although his enemies often argued with him and tried to stop him speaking, Muhammad was able to walk safely around Mecca and preach. Then in the year 619 CE Muhammad suffered two disasters and his situation became desperate. First, his faithful wife Khadija died. Khadija had stood by Muhammad from the beginning and had given him a great deal of support. Her death was a tragic loss. A few months later, Abu Talib, Muhammad's uncle and leader of his family, also died. Although Abu Talib had never accepted Islam, he had given Muhammad the protection of his family and had shown great courage. Another uncle of Muhammad, Abu Lahab, took over the leadership of the family but he refused to protect his nephew. Muhammad's life was now in danger. Because of this he asked some of the clan chiefs who lived outside Mecca for help. Two of the chiefs turned him down but Mutim ibn Adi, chief of the clan of Nawfal, promised to protect him.

Radio Abyssinia: 'Talking Religion: Islam'

Cast: Alexander: Christian interviewer for Radio Abyssinia
Ja'far: One of the Muslims who emigrated from Mecca to Abyssinia
Asma: Ja'far's wife

Scene: Four or five years after Muhammad had begun preaching, life in Mecca had become so dangerous for some of his followers that Muhammad advised them to emigrate to the neighbouring country of Abyssinia (present Ethiopia). About seventy or eighty of the Muslims left Mecca and the Christian King of Abyssinia let them stay in his country. The following is an imaginary radio broadcast. Two Muslims are being interviewed about their beliefs.

ALEXANDER:
(*Interviewer*) Good evening and welcome to yet another programme in our series, 'Talking Religion'. Tonight we have in our studio two Muslims, Ja'far and Asma, both of whom emigrated from Arabia a number of years ago. Thank you both for being with us tonight. We have heard some things about this new religion of yours but I'm sure there is a great deal about Islam we have not understood.

ASMA: Well the first thing to make clear is that Islam is not a *new* religion. Muhammad teaches the same message that was taught by the Prophet Adam.

JA'FAR: There have been many prophets. Some of the most important ones have been Adam, Abraham, Moses and Jesus. All these men taught the belief in one God, but what they said has been forgotten or ignored.

ALEXANDER:
(*Interviewer*) So people who worship many gods, you say, have forgotten the messages of the prophets?

ASMA: Yes, and those who believe in no God...they too ignore the truth.

JA'FAR: People without God think they can live as they please but always it has been true that God is real and that He judges our lives and will reward or punish us.

ASMA: Muhammad tells us that there is nothing more natural than the belief in God. God created all the world and everything in the world worships God. It is only human beings who sometimes think they are so clever and so

23

sure of themselves that they think they can live without God.

ALEXANDER: (*Interviewer*) And Islam teaches that people cannot live without God?

ASMA: That's right...every time we forget about God we make a mess of everything. We fight amongst ourselves, the weak and the sick suffer, we lie and cheat.

JA'FAR: It's only by believing in God and obeying God's will, only then can we live in happiness, only then can we live in peace. Islam means 'submission to God' but it also means 'peace'. In Mecca I knew many wealthy merchants dedicated to making money, but their lives were empty. It is only when they give themselves to God that they will find real happiness.

ALEXANDER: (*Interviewer*) Yes...I think I understand. But, in Islam, how do you give yourself to God? How do you know what God wants?

ASMA: God tells us through the prophets. God told us from the beginning how to live, through the first prophet Adam, and all the prophets since then have said the same thing.

ALEXANDER: (*Interviewer*) Including Muhammad?

JA'FAR Of course, but Muhammad is very special. He is the last prophet God will ever send. After him there will be no others.

ALEXANDER: (*Interviewer*) But if Muhammad is teaching the same thing as Jesus, why don't you all just become Christians? Why do you call yourselves Muslims?

ASMA: There is a great deal Christians and ourselves have in common. We accept everything Jesus taught but we believe Christians have changed most of the things he said. For example, we do not accept the Christian belief that Jesus was God on earth or the Son of God. We would never worship Jesus.

JA'FAR: We say Jesus was certainly a great man, but we do not accept he was God. Nor do we believe Jesus was crucified or resurrected. Jesus was a prophet of God and God would never have let one of His prophets be crucified.

ALEXANDER: (*Interviewer*) Well...there are certainly big differences there. What about your sacred book...the Qur'an? What does the

Qur'an say which makes it so important?

JA'FAR: Well...it tells us how we should live. It is God's guide to us.

ALEXANDER: Oh...I see. That takes us back to what you were saying
(*Interviewer*) earlier on. God tells the people what he wants.

ASMA: Yes...and by obeying what the Qur'an says we will achieve Islam...that is peace.

ALEXANDER: Well, with that I'm afraid we've run out of time. My
(*Interviewer*) thanks to Asma and Ja'far for talking to us this evening. I'm sure there is a great deal more we could learn about Islam, perhaps you could come and speak to us again? Next week we will be back, same time, same channel, with yet another edition of 'Talking Religion'. I hope you will join us. Until then, good night.

What have you remembered?

1. As Islam grew, the chief citizens of Mecca:

took no notice of the Muslims at all	tortured some of the Muslims
encouraged the Muslims to preach their faith	joined Islam in large numbers

2. The name of the black slave who was tortured but who refused to give up was:

| Abu Talib | Ja'far | Abu Bakr | Bilal |

3. Khadija, Muhammad's wife for nearly twenty-five years,

left Muhammad when he started to preach Islam	tried to persuade Muhammad to stop preaching Islam
helped and supported Muhammad all their married life	kept out of the way of Muhammad and let him get on with his preaching

4. To avoid being tortured in Mecca, some seventy or eighty Muslims went to live in:

| Egypt | Syria | Persia | Abyssinia |

5. Muslims believe that there have been many:

| Sons of God | rebirths of Muhammad | Prophets | Daughters of God |

6. The word Islam means 'submission to God' but it also means:

| the religion of Arabia | Peace | idol-worship | the Revelation |

What do you know?

7. Who bought Bilal and gave him his freedom?
8. Apart from Muhammad name four other men who, Muslims believe, were 'prophets'.
9. Explain in what way Christians and Muslims differ in their beliefs about Jesus.
10. What beliefs do Christians and Muslims have in common?

What do you think?

11. Sumaiyya and a number of other Muslims died rather than give up their faith in Islam. A person who does this is called a martyr. Why do you think they put their faith before life itself?
12. Do you think the merchants of Mecca who argued with Muhammad would have put their gods, money and power, before life itself? Try to explain your answer.
13. Imagine you are a radio interviewer and you have to interview two Muslims. Make a list of the questions you would ask. Try to explain why you picked these questions.

The City of the Prophet

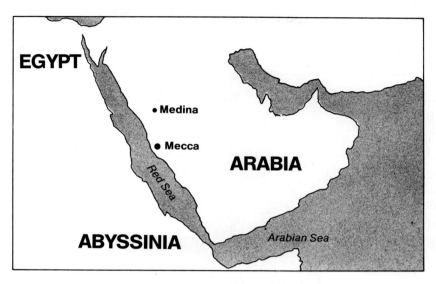

Map showing the location of Medina.
The mosque there contains Muhammad's tomb,
and the tomb of his daughter Fatima.

Ten years after his first revelation there seemed to be little point in Muhammad staying in Mecca. Most of the people in the city continued to oppose him. Why not leave and spread the message of Islam somewhere else? In the year 620 CE, this idea became more than just a possibility. Muhammad met six men from a city called Yathrib which was about three hundred and twenty kilometres north of Mecca. The people of Yathrib were split into two main tribes and there had been a great deal of argument and violence between them. The six men from Yathrib listened with interest to Muhammad. They heard him talk about God, about the revelations of the Qur'an, about the importance of caring for others and about the need for a sense of brotherhood. They felt sure they were hearing the truth. 'This man is God's Prophet,' they said to themselves. 'He is the man we need in our city. Yathrib is divided but with this man's help we could sort out our differences and live in peace.'

Over the next two years the people of Yathrib were to hear a great deal about Muhammad and Islam. In the year 622 CE, after careful planning, Muhammad and his followers left Mecca and went to live in Yathrib. Yathrib was then given a new name...Medina (Madinah). Its full name was *Medinat ul-Nabi*, which means 'the city of the Prophet'. The emigration from Mecca to Medina, or the *Hijrah*, as Muslims call it, marks a vital stage in the growth of Islam. At last, in 'the city of the Prophet', Muhammad could put into practice everything God had told him.

MEDINA MAIL

THE PROPHET ARRIVES SAFELY

Muhammad, Peace be upon him, triumphantly entered Medina yesterday afternoon. Large, jubilant crowds gathered to welcome him and to see the man God has chosen as His final Prophet.

SEARCH PARTIES

It had been feared that the many search parties from Mecca might have stopped Muhammad from reaching Medina, so when he at last arrived loud shouts and cheers went up all over the city. For many months he has been planning this move. Although he could have left long ago, Muhammad bravely stayed on in Mecca, to make sure that all of his followers were able to leave Mecca and arrive safely in Medina.

PLOT

Muhammad himself narrowly survived a plot to kill him before he finally left Mecca. The leaders of Mecca planned to have a group of men, one from each tribe, stab Muhammad to death. God however, protected the Prophet. As the would-be murderers waited all night outside his house, Muhammad was able miraculously to slip past them. To fool them Muhammad's cousin 'Ali, slept that night in Muhammad's bed and it was not until the morning that the team of assassins realised that they had been tricked.

HOW MUHAMMAD MIRACULOUSLY AVOIDED CAPTURE BY THE MECCANS

For full details see CENTRE PAGES.

What the *Mail* says

Medina is rejoicing at Muhammad's arrival and rightly so. God willing, he will bring to an end the bloodshed between the rival tribes and so bring order to this city. He has shown many times a deep sense of justice and an ability to sort out arguments and disagreements amongst people.

ENEMIES

His enemies in Mecca however, could continue to give Muhammad real problems. They seem determined to oppose Muhammad and Islam. Indeed with Muhammad in Medina their best trade routes are threatened. From Medina it would be easy to lead raids against these trade routes. (See map below.)

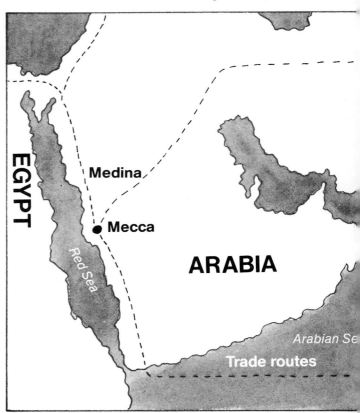

The leaders of Mecca will be angry to see their power limited in this way. They will fight to win it back. Muhammad has always made it clear that he dislikes force but a war with Mecca might be unavoidable.

What have you remembered?

1.	In the year 622 CE, Muhammad and his followers emigrated to the city of
2.	Muslims call the emigration from Mecca to Medina (Yathrib) the
3.	Before Muhammad left Mecca his enemies tried to have him
4.	*Medinat ul-Nabi* means 'the city of the
5.	Based in Medina, the Meccans were afraid Muhammad would raid their

Grid letters (left column): M, H, A, P, T. Additional letter R appears in row T.

What do you know?

6. Ten years after his first revelation why did there seem to be little point in Muhammad staying in Mecca?
7. Before Muhammad went to live in Medina (Yathrib) what was life like in that city?
8. Why did Muhammad wait in Mecca for all of his followers to leave before leaving himself?
9. According to Muslims why did the attempt to kill Muhammad fail?
10. Write an imaginary interview with a leader of Mecca (i.e. Abu Jahl, see pages 18–20) in which he explains what he thinks the Meccans should do now that Muhammad is in Medina.

What do you think?

11. Why do you think the merchants of Mecca wanted Muhammad dead?
12. The people of Medina (Yathrib) invited Muhammad to live in their city and they were very pleased when he finally arrived. Why do you think they wanted him so much in their city? What do you think they hoped he would do for their city?
13. From what you know about Muhammad when he lived in Mecca make a list of his best qualities. Which of these qualities do you most admire? Try to explain why.
14. What do you think it was about Islam that the followers of Muhammad found most attractive?

UNIT 6
Victory at Badr

As soon as Muhammad arrived in Medina, he began to make changes. Muhammad had said that too many people were greedy and unjust. In Medina things were going to be different. Muhammad encouraged the Medinan and the Meccan Muslims to work together. They built a place, a mosque, in which all Muslims could worship. Gradually, the people forgot their differences and learnt to live happily together as one community.

'Say (O Muhammad): O my people!
Work according to your power.
Lo! I too am working...'
(The Qur'an, Surah 6, verse 136.)

However, Muhammad knew that the Muslims could not enjoy peace as long as the leaders of Mecca were against him. If the Muslims did not fight to defend themselves then they would suffer a great deal. War between Mecca and Medina seemed impossible to avoid. In the first year of Muhammad's arrival in Medina there was a number of clashes between Meccan idol-worshippers and Muslims, but the first real battle between the two cities took place nearly eighteen months after Muhammad had left Mecca. This was the battle of Badr.

The Arabian Broadcasting Company: ABC

Cast:

Layla:	News presenter/interviewer	
Hamama:	News reporter	
Colonel Hashim:	Retired army commander	
Sahla:	Political correspondent for the *Medina Mail*	

LAYLA:
(*News presenter*)

Reports are coming through of a battle now being fought between an army from Mecca and an army of Muslims led by Muhammad. For an eye-witness account of what is happening we go over to our reporter at the battle, Hamama.

HAMAMA:
(*News reporter*)

An extraordinary victory is taking place before my very eyes. The army from Mecca of over nine hundred men are being forced back by the Muslim army of only three hundred. It's almost impossible to believe. A short time ago Hamza and 'Ali led the Muslims in a fierce charge. In all my years as a war correspondent I've never seen an attack quite like it. These Muslims seem to have no fear. They rushed into what seemed certain death, slashing ruthlessly with their swords and it now looks as if the Meccan army are on the run...yes, they're running away. This is going to be a complete victory for Muhammad. It's just incredible...

LAYLA:
(*News presenter*)

Well...I'm afraid we've lost contact with Hamama. While we are trying to sort that out I am able to speak to a very experienced army commander, Colonel Hashim, and to Sahla, who is of course the political correspondent for the *Medina Mail*. Can either of you explain what has happened today? Why has Mecca lost this battle? Colonel Hashim, what do you think?

COLONEL HASHIM: This is a terrible defeat for Mecca and it's obvious that a number of blunders have been made...the lack of water being one of them. The Meccan army, after their long desert march, had little water and they must have been exhausted but Muhammad cleverly prevented them from getting to the water wells at Badr.

SAHLA: Yes, but the Muslims have won this victory for other reasons, apart from Muhammad's clever tactics. This victory is a miracle from God. God's angels fought alongside the Muslims.

COLONEL HASHIM: That's as maybe, but certainly Muhammad is able to fill his men with amazing courage. That charge of the Muslim army, for instance.

LAYLA: Death doesn't frighten them does it?

COLONEL HASHIM: Their faith is a big factor here. They believe that if they die in battle they will live again in paradise. Morale and the belief in what one is fighting for is essential if an army is to win.

SAHLA: But I repeat, much more important than their morale or Muhammad's leadership, is their faith in God. It is because of their faith, that God has given victory to the Muslims today.

COLONEL HASHIM: Well, if that's true, the Meccans had better watch out.

LAYLA: Thank you Sahla and Colonel Hashim. From the battle we have reports that fifty to seventy Meccans are dead whereas only fourteen Muslims are dead. With that news we return to our scheduled programme.

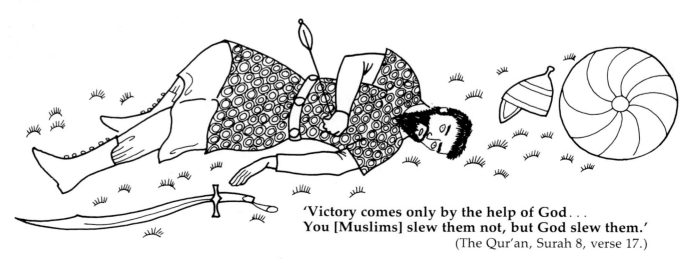

'Victory comes only by the help of God...
You [Muslims] slew them not, but God slew them.'
(The Qur'an, Surah 8, verse 17.)

What have you remembered?

Answer the following questions and complete the word puzzle.

1. Muhammad said that too many people were

2. Muhammad encouraged the Muslims in Medina to live together as a

3. In the first year of Muhammad's stay in Medina there was a number of these against Mecca

4. After the battle of Badr many of Muhammad's worst enemies were now

5. At the battle of Badr Muhammad was heavily

6. Medina was to be a city in which who could live?

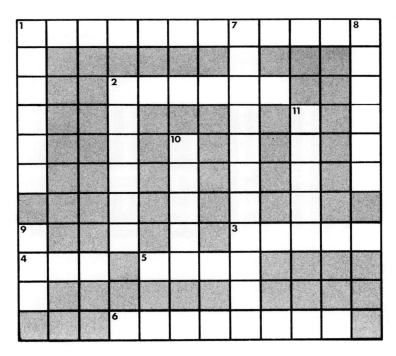

CLUES ACROSS

1. At the battle of Badr Muhammad had this number in his army.
2. Muhammad left Mecca and went to live in this city.
3. In battle the Muslims seemed to have no fear even of this.
4. He showed great courage at the battle of Badr.
5. The first main battle Muhammad had to fight.
6. The Muslims believed that if they died fighting for Islam they would be rewarded here in an afterlife.

CLUES DOWN

1. The number of years from Muhammad's first revelation until he left Mecca.
2. The place in which the Muslims worshipped.
7. At the battle of Badr the army the Muslims fought was this big.
8. Before Badr the Meccan army had a long march through this.
9. Muhammad didn't want this but if the Muslims in Medina were to survive it could not be avoided.
10. The city in which Muhammad's enemies lived.
11. He showed great courage at the battle of Badr.

What do you know?

8. In the imaginary interview, how does Colonel Hashim explain the victory of the Muslims at the battle of Badr?
9. Muhammad wanted life in Medina to be very different from life in Mecca. What were some of the ways in which Muhammad wanted Medina to be different?
10. Why did Muhammad believe he had to fight against his enemies in Mecca? What did he believe would happen to Islam if he didn't fight?
11. In other major world religions there are several famous religious leaders who, like Muhammad, were involved in battles. Can you name two such leaders?

What do you think?

12. At the battle of Badr the Muslims were heavily outnumbered but of the victory the Qur'an says, 'Victory comes only by the help of God . . . You [Muslims] slew them not, but God slew them.' Imagine you are interviewing a Muslim who fought at the battle. How do you think he would explain the victory?
13. Do you think war is ever justified? Try to explain your answer.

The Years of Growth

The battle of Badr was a great victory for Muhammad. Some of his worst enemies had been killed and the Muslims had proved they could defend themselves. However, the war between Mecca and Medina was not over. There were still many in Mecca who wanted revenge and Muhammad and his followers had to fight two more battles against them. During these battles the Muslims were greatly outnumbered and yet their enemies were unable to kill Muhammad or to capture Medina.

Although a lot of Muhammad's time was taken up with the war against Mecca, he continued to teach Islam and to help his followers to understand more about God. Muhammad and his followers also visited people in more distant places. Many of these people found that what Muhammad had to say made sense and so they too became Muslims.

'And those who believe and do good works and believe in that which is revealed unto Muhammad...'
(The Qur'an, Surah 47, verse 2.)

Islam is Heard

Cast: Abu Bara: The tribal chief of the Beni Aamir
           Raihana: The daughter of Abu Bara
              Bilal: A Muslim and an ex-slave, who was tortured
                        in Mecca
       Sa'd ibn Ubada: A Muslim and a chief citizen of Medina

Scene: The camp of the desert tribe Beni Aamir. Inside Abu Bara's tent.

ABU BARA: Come in, gentlemen. You've come a long way.

RAIHANA: Father! You're not really going to speak to these men?

ABU BARA: Don't be ridiculous, Raihana. Where are your manners?

SA'D: If it's awkward we'll go.

ABU BARA: No...Raihana's just a little headstrong. Please...sit
             down. Tell me the news in Medina. I hear extraordinary
             things have been happening.

SA'D: Marvellous things have been happening. We no longer
         argue amongst ourselves. At last we have a strong leader
         who we all respect.

RAIHANA: Huh...Muhammad, the madman from Mecca!

BILAL: Muhammad once said, 'Abuse nobody, and if a man
          abuses you do not abuse him in return.' Are those the
          words of a madman?

ABU BARA: This Muhammad is obviously clever but what is he like?

SA'D: I've never known a man like him. He is never proud or
         boastful.

BILAL: He's deeply religious. Frequently, he will spend all night
          in prayer. He also visits the sick.

SA'D: He lives in just a simple house which he helped to build
         himself.

BILAL: He could live like a king in Medina but he doesn't. He
          lives on dates and camel's milk mainly.

ABU BARA: Doesn't he have money?

SA'D: He never spends money on himself. People give him
         money but he then gives it away to widows, orphans, the
         sick, the poor — anybody who needs help.

BILAL: Muhammad says, 'Riches are not from worldly goods, but
          from a contented mind.' You should meet him, Abu Bara.

He's so strong and determined and yet so kind and gentle. The people go to him all the time for advice but he never refuses to listen. He even finds time to play with the children.

RAIHANA: That's all very well but the things he says can't work. Why...if he could, he would free all the slaves! You yourself are an ex-slave, freed because of Muhammad.

BILAL: Of course he would free the slaves. Only God is our master, not another man. That's why Muhammad gives rights to women. Some men treat their wives like slaves. Muhammad says husbands should look after their wives and not beat them as if they were animals. Muhammad does odd jobs around the house and patches his own clothes.

ABU BARA: That's undignified work for a man.

SA'D: Muhammad gives it dignity and he gives women dignity as well. He says we should not divorce our wives and he has given them the right to inherit some of the wealth of their husbands.

RAIHANA: Now that I agree with. There are too many men who divorce their wives for no reason, after years of marriage. They throw them out like a worn-out carpet.

SA'D: Medina is more happy and prosperous than I've ever known it. There is little violence or crime in the city but if someone does do something wrong they are punished according to the law we have from God. A shopkeeper can leave the market to worship in the mosque and he will not be robbed.

BILAL: Muslims are brothers and sisters, and one doesn't steal from one's family. Sa'd here is an Arab nobleman and one of the leaders of his tribe, whereas I'm an ex-slave, yet we travel, talk, eat and worship together.

SA'D: Why don't you join us, Abu Bara? Become a Muslim.

ABU BARA: No, not yet. You must give me time to think.

RAIHANA: Father...you can't be serious!

ABU BARA: Why not Raihana? I can see even you are impressed. There is too much injustice in this country and there are too many for whom life is empty and without meaning. Perhaps this man Muhammad has the answer.

BILAL: It is God who has the answer.

ABU BARA: Maybe so. Gentlemen...I must rest now. Tell Muhammad that I would like to meet him soon, and that perhaps I will give him permission to teach Islam to my tribe.

'They ask thee (Muhammad), what they shall spend. Say: That which ye spend for good [must go] to parents and near kindred and orphans and the wayfarer...'
(The Qur'an, Surah 2, verse 215.)

What have you remembered?

1. In Medina Muhammad lived in

| a huge palace | a simple house | a strong fortress | the Ka'ba |

2. When Muhammad was living in Medina there was

| frequent violence in the city | an increase in the number of slaves |

| little violence or crime in the city | an outbreak of sickness |

3. After a revelation of the Qur'an, Muhammad

| took away all rights for women | gave special rights to the Merchants |

| gave idol worshippers special rights | gave women special rights |

4. Muhammad said, 'Abuse nobody...

| ...and if a man abuses you abuse him in return.' | ...but if a man abuses you strike him across the face.' |

| ...but save your curses for the idol worshippers.' | ...and if a man abuses you do not abuse him in return.' |

5. Muhammad said, 'Riches are not from worldly goods, but from...

| ...a steady job.' | ...a wealthy friend.' |

| ...a contented mind.' | ...a cunning mind.' |

What do you know?

6. The people of Medina gave Muhammad money. How did he use it?
7. What special instructions did Muhammad give to husbands about how they should treat their wives?
8. Muhammad's life was always simple and non-luxurious. In two areas of his life, his food and clothing, explain how Muhammad preferred to keep his life simple.
9. In the imaginary play, 'Islam is Heard', Sa'd says Muhammad was 'never proud or boastful'. What examples can you find in the play of Muhammad's modesty?
10. When Muhammad lived in Medina there was little crime. In the imaginary play, 'Islam is Heard' what reason does Bilal give for this?

What do you think?

Many people who heard Muhammad speak thought that his words were full of such truth that they wrote down many of his sayings. The revelations Muslims believe Muhammad received from God are written down in the Qur'an but Muhammad's sayings and actions are recorded in writings called the Hadith. Below are just some of the sayings of Muhammad.

'The one who looks after a widow or a poor person is like a warrior who fights for God's cause, or like one who performs prayers all the night and fasts all the day.'

'Do not shut your money bag otherwise God too will with hold His blessings from you. Spend in God's cause as much as you can.'

'The ink of the scholar is more holy than the blood of the martyr.'

'Acquire knowledge. It enables its possessor to distinguish right from wrong; it lighteth the way to Heaven; it is our friend in the desert, our society in solitude, our companion when friendless; it guides us to happiness; it sustains us in misery; it is an ornament amongst friends, and an armour against enemies.'

'Treat the people with ease and don't be hard on them; give them glad tiding and don't fill them with hatred; and love each other, and don't differ.'

11. Which one of these sayings do you like most?
12. Explain what you think the saying is about.
13. Try to explain why you like it.
14. Muhammad said that wealth could not buy happiness. How true do you think this is?
15. Do you think many people today believe that wealth can bring real happiness? What do you think brings real happiness in life?

UNIT 8

Triumph at Last

When Muhammad left Mecca to live in Medina he had only a few supporters and yet six years later Islam had grown enormously. During those six years Muhammad had explained the meaning of Islam to as many people as possible. People from all over Arabia had become Muslims but the citizens of Mecca still refused to accept the faith.

Even so, Muhammad longed to visit Mecca and worship God at the Ka'ba. To make such a pilgrimage was unthinkable. Unthinkable that is until, in a revelation, God told him to go. Convinced that God had commanded him, Muhammad hurriedly prepared and it was not long before he and a thousand of his followers set off for Mecca. The year was 628 CE. They all knew that the journey was highly dangerous. Dressed as pilgrims they were easy victims for the Meccans. Nevertheless, they travelled safely towards Mecca and camped about twelve kilometres outside the city in a valley called Hudaibiyah. Muhammad sent a message into the city saying, 'I have not come to fight but to make a pilgrimage to the Ka'ba' and then waited to see what would happen. Tension mounted in the Muslim camp. Would the Meccans attack them? Would they be allowed into the city? Many of Muhammad's friends could not understand why they had come to Mecca in this way. Why come as pilgrims? Why risk the lives of so many?

'Lo! We have given thee
(O Muhammad) a signal victory.'
(The Qur'an, Surah 48, verse 1.)

Muhammad's decision to go to Mecca seemed pointless and far too dangerous but his actions amazed many of the people of Mecca. They knew that Muhammad was waiting, unarmed, outside their city and so could not be a real threat. Many Meccans at last realised that this meant that Muhammad did not want war and that he would not destroy the Ka'ba. The following day, instead of attacking Muhammad the Meccans agreed a peace treaty with him.

The peace treaty signed at Hudaibiyah was a great victory for the Muslims. It allowed them to go on pilgrimage to Mecca the next year and every year after that. It also meant that the war between Mecca and Medina was over and Muhammad and his followers could now preach Islam all over Arabia. Because Muslims were now free to spread the message, Islam grew more quickly than ever. But still the people of Mecca refused to accept the faith.

'...**There is no God save Him, the Almighty, the Wise. He it is Who hath revealed unto thee [Muhammad] the Scripture wherein are clear revelations.'**
(The Qur'an, Surah 3, verses 6–7.)

For two years the peace agreed at Hudaibiyah worked well but then the Meccans broke the treaty. A group of Muslims was attacked and one of them was killed. The incident could not be ignored. Now was the time for Muhammad to take control of Mecca. With an army of over 10 000 men he marched on the city and captured it with virtually no bloodshed. Islam had now triumphed.

For two more years Muhammad lived in Medina, keeping his promise never to desert the city. People went to the city from all over Arabia, swearing support for Muhammad and Islam. But, in the year 632 CE, Muhammad fell seriously ill. He probably had pneumonia, although some people at the time thought he had been poisoned. Whatever the cause of his illness, he was never to recover. At the age of sixty-two, after twenty-three years of successfully teaching Islam and converting most of his countrymen and women, the great prophet died. He was buried in the mosque that he himself had helped to build in Medina, and today millions of Muslims visit his tomb and pay their respects to one of the world's great leaders of religion.

The Entry into Mecca
The Arabian Broadcasting Company: ABC

Cast: Hassan: A news reporter for ABC
           Zainab: A news reporter for ABC
   Abu Sufyan: A rich merchant and one of the main leaders of Mecca
          Sofiya: An expert on Islam

Scene: 630 CE. Mecca.

HASSAN:
(News reporter)

This is ABC News coming to you live from Mecca. You join us as Muhammad makes his triumphant entry into Mecca with an army of over 10 000 men. The atmosphere is very tense but it doesn't look as if this army will fight today. Muhammad's support throughout the country is so great that it would surely be suicidal for Mecca to try to resist him.

We go over now to our roving camera and to Zainab who is in the crowd. Hello Zainab, I see you have with you Abu Sufyan. Abu Sufyan is one of the leaders of Mecca and for twenty years has been an enemy of Islam.

ZAINAB:
(News reporter)

Abu Sufyan, I know this must be a difficult time for you but could I ask you a few questions? I understand you spoke to Muhammad early this morning. What did he say?

ABU SUFYAN:

I wanted to know if he intended to attack Mecca. He told me that he did not want to fight or take lives. He promised that if Mecca surrendered peacefully no one would be injured.

ZAINAB:
(News reporter)

Do you think he will keep his word?

ABU SUFYAN:

I would not blame him if he didn't. Over the years we have ambushed, tortured and killed hundreds of his supporters. We have been particularly cruel with Muslim prisoners of war, but if there is one thing I have learned about Muhammad it is that he always keeps his word.

ZAINAB:
(News reporter)

We have reports that Muhammad has dismissed one of his army commanders, Sa'd ibn Ubada, and has replaced him with 'Ali. What do you think is the significance of this?

ABU SUFYAN: This is a good sign I think. Sa'd has been taking a hard line, saying that I and a number of other Meccan leaders should be executed. Muhammad, on the other hand, wants this to be a day of peace and I'm sure he will get his way.

ZAINAB:
(*News reporter*) Thank you, Abu Sufyan. We return now to Hassan. Is Muhammad getting his own way, Hassan? Is the entry still non-violent?

HASSAN:
(*News reporter*) Pretty much so, although a skirmish has taken place in southwest Mecca. A column of Muhammad's army was attacked by a group of Meccans. This was quickly dealt with but twelve of the Meccans have died. Muhammad has appealed for calm. Muhammad has now arrived at the Ka'ba. With us in the studio we have Sofiya who will help us to understand what is going on. Sofiya, does Muhammad intend to destroy the Ka'ba?

SOFIYA:
(*Islam expert*) Not at all. For Muslims the Ka'ba is the most ancient and holiest shrine in the world. This is the shrine they believe Abraham built hundreds of years ago. However, since the days of Abraham the Ka'ba has been corrupted. The false gods that the Meccans keep in the Ka'ba should not be there.

HASSAN:
(*News reporter*) Muhammad has now opened the door of the Ka'ba. He's turning to the crowd. . .he's saying something. . .I missed that. . .what did he say?

SOFIYA:
(*Islam expert*) He's quoting from the Qur'an, 'The truth has come and falsehood has passed away; verily falsehood is sure to pass away.'

HASSAN:
(*News reporter*) He's now having the statues of the gods brought out of the Ka. . .good grief. . .with his staff he's knocking over the statues of the gods. He seems to have no fear of the gods.

SOFIYA:
(*Islam expert*) Of course not. Muhammad has always said that these aren't gods at all but just wood and stone.

HASSAN:
(*News reporter*) Muhammad has issued orders and a fire has been lit and all the broken statues are being collected and burnt.

SOFIYA:
(*Islam expert*) For Muslims there could be no better demonstration that these gods are false than what we are seeing today. This is the purification of the Ka'ba and now this building will become what it was intended to be. . .the central shrine of God.

HASSAN: Muhammad is now turning to all the chief citizens of Mecca...all of his enemies who have fought against him for twenty years. Muhammad is saying to them, 'What do you think I am about to do with you?' This is it...will he have them all beheaded?...Well, that is extraordinary. Muhammad has set them all free! 'Go your way,' he said, 'for you are the freed ones.'

SOFIYA:
(*Islam expert*) They can hardly believe it, can they, and yet magnanimity is something that Muhammad has always encouraged in his followers.

HASSAN:
(*News reporter*) Bilal, the ex-slave, is now calling the people to prayer. Muhammad's vast army have put down their weapons and are now silent in prayer. And so, with the news that Muhammad has taken Mecca virtually with no bloodshed and has let all his old enemies go free, we end this news broadcast.

'And seek forgiveness of God.
Lo! God is ever forgiving and merciful.'
(The Qur'an, Surah 4, verse 106.)

What have you remembered?

Complete the sentences. Match the phrases in the left-hand column with the phrases from the right.

1.	Muhammad's journey to Mecca in 628 CE was	captured it with virtually no bloodshed
2.	With Muhammad waiting unarmed outside their city, many Meccans realised	go on pilgrimage
3.	The peace treaty signed at Hudaibiyah made it easier for the Muslims to	ill and died
4.	The peace treaty signed at Hudaibiyah made it possible for the Muslims to	highly dangerous
5.	With an army of over 10 000 men Muhammad marched on Mecca and	preach Islam all over Arabia
6.	In the year 632 CE Muhammad fell seriously	that Muhammad did not want war

What do you know?

7. Why was Muhammad's attempted pilgrimage to Mecca in 628 CE so dangerous?

8. What might Muhammad's decision to go to Mecca in 628 CE have helped many of the people of Mecca to realise?

9. The scene is the Muslim camp in the valley of Hudaibiyah. It is night and two Muslims are keeping warm around a fire. They are discussing whether Muhammad should have brought them on pilgrimage. Write an imaginary conversation which the two men might have had.

10. When Muhammad captured Mecca he did not destroy the Ka'ba shrine itself. What did he destroy?

11. In the imaginary broadcast, 'The Entry into Mecca', we are told that Muhammad dismissed one of his army commanders, Sa'd ibn Ubada. By doing this what was Muhammad hoping to ensure?

12. Magnanimity is something that Muhammad always encouraged in his followers. What does 'magnanimity' mean? Write a short story in which the meaning of magnanimity is made clear.

What do you think?

13. Although many people expected him to, Muhammad did not have his enemies executed. What do you think this tells us about Muhammad's character?

'There is no god but God
and Muhammad is His Prophet.'

Muhammad's death was a great blow to many of his followers. Some could not believe he was dead — they thought he would live forever. When rumours of his death began to spread, many in Medina went almost berserk, shouting and arguing. It was Muhammad's closest friend, Abu Bakr, who brought order to the city. He stood up in the mosque and said quietly, 'O men, if anyone worships Muhammad, let him know that Muhammad is dead. But if anyone worships God, let him know that God is alive and immortal for ever.'

These brief words sum up an important belief Muslims have about Muhammad. Muslims do not worship Muhammad. They worship God and God only. This is one of the reasons why Muslims would never draw, paint or carve an image of Muhammad. They would not allow an actor to play his part in a film or play. To draw a picture of Muhammad might be the first step towards worshipping him. It would turn him into an idol, and worshipping idols was the very thing Muhammad was most against.

For Muslims, Muhammad is God's Prophet and the Messenger of God. He was not God Himself, or the Son of God. Muhammad was a man. Muslims believe there have been many prophets, but Muhammad is very special because he is the last and finest prophet to be sent by God. This is why Muhammad is often called 'the Seal of the Prophets'. To most Muslims, Muhammad is simply called 'the Prophet'. Whenever his name is used, as a mark of the deep respect they have towards him, Muslims always follow it with the Arabic words, 'Sal-lal-Lahu Alyhe wa Sallam', which means, 'may God's blessing and salutation be upon him'.

Muhammad is thought of as the perfect prophet and he is also seen as the perfect man, whose way of life and character are an example to everyone. He is also regarded as the perfect ruler and statesman. The Muslim community he created at Medina is the example which all Muslim communities should strive to be like. Millions of Muslims over the years have carefully modelled their lives on his life. They have tried to be as generous, courageous and kind as he was and they have also copied the minute details of his life such as the way he worshipped, washed, dressed and ate.

For Muslims Muhammad is the 'most noble of all creation' and of him the Qur'an says. 'Lo God and his angels shower blessings on the Prophet. O ye who believe! Ask blessings on him and salute him with a worthy salutation,' (The Qur'an, Surah 33, verse 56).

'Praise be to God, Lord of the Worlds.'
(The Qur'an, Surah 1, verse 1.)